Finding Your Own
Voice in Academic
Publishing

Writing Your Way to Success

Susan M. Drake & Glen A. Jones

NEW
FORUMS
Stillwater, Oklahoma
U.S.A.

NEW FORUMS PRESS INC.

Published in the United States of America
by New Forums Press, Inc.1018 S. Lewis St.
Stillwater, OK 74074
www.newforums.com

Copyright © 1997 by New Forums Press, Inc.

All rights reserved. No part of this publication may be reproduced or transmitted in any form or by any means, electronic or mechanical, including photocopy, or any information storage or retrieval system, without permission in writing from the publisher.

Library of Congress Cataloging-in-Publication Data Pending

This book may be ordered in bulk quantities at discount from New Forums Press, Inc., P.O. Box 876, Stillwater, OK 74076 [Federal I.D. No. 73 1123239]. Printed in the United States of America.

ISBN 10: 0-913507-63-6

Table of Contents

Introduction v

Our Stories 1
Susan's Writing Path 1
Glen's Writing Path 2

Why Write? 5

Choosing A Focus 9
Traditional Approaches 10
Revisiting a Thesis 10
Working on a Collaborative Project 11
Action Research 12
Book Reviews 13
Books 14

Finding the Right Journal 17
Creating a Personalized Data Base 17
Other Avenues 19
Rule of Three 20
Dealing with Rejection 21

Writing Your Way To Clarity 23

On Being Clear and Accessible2 5

Getting Started 27

Exploring the Literature 31
  Data Bases 32
  Snowball Approach 33
  Reviewing Systematically 34
  Reviewing With the Computer 35
Organizing for Clarity 37
  Clarity of Purpose 38
  Editing 41

Journal Editors and Editorial Boards 43

Maintaining Self Motivation 49
  Accept Rejection as Inevitable 49
  Stick to a Routine 50
  Volunteer to Teach a New Course 50
  Present a Workshop in Somewhat Unfamiliar Territory 51
  Send in Proposals for Conferences 51
  Identify and Prioritize 51
  Goal Setting 52

Life After Publication 53

Conclusion 55

References 57

Introduction

THERE ARE MANY BOOKS available that will guide the academic to substantive academic writing (Simon, 1994; Moxley, 1992; Boice, 1990; Luey, 1990.) However, according to Robert Boice, a well known authority on writing, approximately 85% of publications are written by 15% of the academic population. Many academics experience the writing process as very difficult and painful. As a result, they give up writing rather than try to surmount the obstacles. This monograph takes a fresh look at the publishing game and offers tried and true strategies that allowed two new academics to experience publishing success. It is hoped that by offering these strategies other academics may reframe and refocus their writing endeavors to facilitate more ease in the writing process and therefore to experience greater success in academic publishing.

Our Stories

WE ARE NOT WIDELY known publishing stars. Rather, we are two Canadian early career professors of education. Susan is just completing her fifth year, Glen his second. We have both experienced the tensions of being new professors and the "publish or perish" phenomena. Although we would be the first to admit that these can be daunting experiences, we also have found our way through the maze of life in academia. We have both been able to establish a publication record, and advace to the rank of Associate Professor. In analyzing this success, we believe we can offer some strategies to help others navigate the bumpy journey to successful academic publishing.

Both of us travelled a different route to being published. We have different philosophies, work habits and academic interests. Yet we both have come to believe that we can write and we have something worth writing about. Since our paths to this realization have been different, we often will differentiate between Susan's and Glen's experiences. At times the suggestions put forward may seem contradictory, as often diverse approaches have worked for us in like situations. At other times we will write with a single voice. We hope our readers will find their own voice within the pages ahead.

Susan's Writing Path

For twenty years, Susan taught in a high school setting before returning to graduate school to do a doctorate in curriculum. Being a physical education teacher, she had spent much of her spare time in the coaching arena and writing was certainly not a part of this lifestyle. During this period spent in schools, however, she developed a strong philosophy of teaching based on her real life experiences. Although Susan was consistently seeking out professional development through seminars and workshops, theory was not a part of her day to day life in the classroom. She had come to rely on her "experienced wisdom" gained through her own experiences as the best guide for classroom practice.

On returning to graduate school, Susan left behind the world of physical and health education to study learning foundations for her masters degree and curriculum for her doctorate. She became immersed in educational theory. Here she was delighted to find theories that she could connect to her own experience. She was also presented with a multitude of theories that did not fit. This was a completely new experience from her undergraduate days when she had found herself bouncing from theory to theory, captivated by each author's presentation and unable to write a substantive critique that expressed her own voice. In hindsight, she realized that when she was an undergraduate the theorist had been the expert; she had been the student passively absorbing information. It was an exciting time, as a graduate student, to be able to write required term papers from the ground of her own experiences. Fortunately she was able to substantiate her work with current theory that supported her ideas.

For Susan, finding her own voice and learning to express it in an academic framework has been the underlying route to success both at graduate school and as a new professor. It has not been an entirely easy path; like other academics struggling to develop a publication record, Susan has had her share of rejections and setbacks. Still, she has come to learn that when she writes with an authentic voice she can find a forum in which to be heard, and she has also learned that writing from the place of her deepest beliefs is definitely worth the struggle. Her story then is framed in an "inside out" approach to writing and publication.

Glen's Writing Path

Glen has always been interested in people and the way in which they work together within organizations. While completing undergraduate programs in political science and education, he became extremely involved in university governance. It was through this experience that he gained an interest in understanding how universities work and he decided to pursue graduate studies in the field of higher education. The courses and research he completed for his doctorate provided him with an opportunity to reflect on the relationship between his prior experience and the theories and ideas expressed in the research literature. It was an incredibly positive experience.

Part way through his doctoral program, Glen and a colleague attended an important academic conference and had an opportunity to meet quite a number of other graduate students. One of the common themes that emerged from the meeting was the tremendous importance of publication in academic life. Glen and his friend concluded that they should begin to enter the world of scholarly publishing as soon as possible. Their discussions with other graduate students who were already publishing convinced them that all it would really take was a few ideas and some hard work. Within two years both Glen and his colleague had published several articles.

While still a graduate student, Glen created a new academic journal and gained important experience in the editorial side of the enterprise. Aside from his own writing activities, Glen now sits on the editorial boards of two journals, is an executive member of a national scholarly association, and has been involved in the organization of several academic conferences. He views these activities as a natural extension of his interest in organizations and structures–of understanding how things work. There is little doubt that learning about the operation of scholarly journals has also given him a new perspective on how his own writing fits into the broader context of scholarly publication and the dissemination of knowledge.

Glen enjoys writing. He views the process as an intellectual exercise, a forum for pulling together the ideas and thoughts that he has been playing with into a form that can be understood by others. While he is particularly fond of the creative side of the writing process, he is also cognizant that he cannot always rely on his creative energies to see projects through to completion and he has experimented with different strategies to ensure that he finishes every project that he starts.

Glen's story, then, is based on the various strategies he has found useful in the writing process, and his understanding of how editors and editorial boards work and make decisions.

Why Write?

ANYONE WHO ENTERS the academic arena is struck by the perceived need to write. The "publish or perish" phenomenon is an all too real threat. As well, at many faculties there seems to be a flurry of activity surrounding research and writing that the new academic does not feel connected to and can find intimidating.

How realistic is the need to get published? From our perspective as new professors, the need was very real. As well, it seemed that the criteria to acquire and keep a job in higher education have increased since the days our more experienced colleagues entered the profession. Thus, it seemed that the number of articles we could write and get "in press" was never enough to be quite good enough. Much of our perceived pressure came from an internal source. At some point, enough was enough–but we could never quite know when that was. Both of us were driven then by the haunting phrase of "publish or perish."

Our reaction to the pressure of the academic culture to publish is only one way to respond. Many of our colleagues seem to react by becoming paralyzed by the process. They claim they can find nothing worth writing about, or there is too little time, or the writing process itself is too difficult. Much of their time is devoured by teaching, attending committee meetings and counselling needy students. There is little time for thinking about research, and even less for writing about it. These are very realistic responses; however, they can become terrifying if a lack of publications can lead to loss of a job or the inability to get tenure. Although we certainly can identify with these dilemmas, we believe that sometimes drowning in the tasks of everyday academia can provide an escape from facing the challenge of writing. We believe there are ways to get beyond the "publishing imperative" that will allow academics to begin to enjoy the writing process itself.

In spite of a general tendency to avoid writing, there are

many personal and professional rewards that accompany getting published. First there is a sense of satisfaction when one gets to a place where the "writing is easy". Susan now experiences a sense of relief when she returns to her writing after an extended period away from it. But this feeling came as a surprise and has only come over time. Still, it feels good to get ideas down on paper and to continue reworking them until they flow in some logical sequence. Glen views writing as a very important part of academic work. He has found that there are many external rewards associated with publication, but there are also important internal rewards. Writing provides a form of closure for the research process, and he continues to learn more about himself and his ideas with each new project.

Yet, it is the professional rewards that have surprised us. Susan offered workshops and gave public addresses for many years before she felt "forced" to write her ideas for publication. Once her ideas appeared in written form she was startled by how much more attention they received as compared to oral communication. She learned the tremendous power of the written word. Although she had always suspected that few people read journal articles, she regularly receives phone calls or letters from people who have read her work and would like to discuss the ideas further. This has allowed her a rich network of people with similar interests both in the field of education and in academia. This positive result has been a most rewarding and unexpected professional bonus.

Like Susan, Glen has found that his writing has increased his network of academic contacts. These new contacts often led to new and interesting outlets for his writing. While his first seven or eight papers appeared in peer reviewed journals, he now finds that an increasing amount of his writing concerns pieces commissioned by others, including chapters for edited books and essays for reference works. The more he writes, the more he finds that he is presented with opportunities to do new things in the publishing world: to review articles for new journals, write reviews, sit on editorial boards, and write commissioned pieces that provide him with the freedom to stray from the traditional structures of the "research article." In other words, he believes that writing opens up tremendous new opportunities for scholars and increases the breadth of choices available to them in determining how they will build their careers.

Choosing A Focus

ONE OF THE HARDEST THINGS to do is to choose a focus to write about. This difficult decision can offer a powerful writing block and create an impasse to any writing ahead. The time honored choices seem to be traditional research, reviews of the literature or book reviews. This can seem daunting if one is beginning from scratch. We believe that you should write about what intrigues you. To find the right topic begins with a hard look at ourselves. What is it that is important to us? What do we believe is important for others to know? Where do we spend our energy? What energizes us? Susan was told by well meaning others to abandon the track she was pursuing because "although it was interesting, it did not have enough rigor and would not be accepted by academic journals." Fortunately, Susan listened to her own voice here and continued to write about what most intrigued her. Eventually, this work was accepted in many forums.

In searching for the "right" topic to write about, the first place to look is at what interests you most. This may not be your professed area of expertise. Rather, it may be a flaw that you have spotted in some current theory. Try out your ideas with your students. Their reaction to your work will offer a good clue as to how it might be received in the academic community. It is important to recognize that the divisions between fields of study (and in a similar way, between journals) can be quite arbitrary. There is nothing inappropriate in using ideas and approaches associated with one discipline or field to discuss a topic associated with another field. In some cases an interdisciplinary approach can open up completely new ways of looking at particular questions and suggest new types of writing and different forums for publication.

It is important to recognize that there is a wide variety of approaches or types of writing in addition to the form that is traditionally used in your field. You have to decide how you will approach your topic, but we strongly encourage you to consider a wide range of options in addition to, or instead of, the traditional form associated with your field. Experimenting with different forms and approaches can be an exciting and enlightening part of the writing process.

We think that there are ways to ease into the writing process that can make the transition into "writer" smoother. However, the ideas we suggest are not for everyone and thus we recommend that the writer go with the strategies that seem intrinsically interesting.

Traditional Approaches

In most fields of study there is a traditional form or approach. In many branches of the social sciences, for example, this approach involves reporting on a research project. You may want to ask a specific question and write a traditional article based on original research, but it would be a mistake to assume that this is the only approach that will lead to publication.

Some journals specialize in literature reviews where the author attempts to synthesize the work that has already been published on the topic. This sort of approach can present a wonderful opportunity to shape how others view the field and to introduce your own ideas and your personal reflections on the subject.

Some journals welcome public debates between scholars. Rather than conduct a new study in the field, you might decide to critique a recent article and use that approach as a means of introducing new ideas to the field or to questioning assumptions that appear in the work of others.

Revisiting a Thesis

New scholars have often just completed a thesis, and usually believe that they should write about some aspect of it. After all, they have spent a good part of their life investigating this topic and they know a great deal more about it than anyone else. Looking to a thesis for generating writing ideas can be a good starting point. A self appointed mentor recommended that Susan try to publish her entire thesis if she wanted to carve out a successful career path. However, not everyone can go this route (and Susan herself only published a part of hers). Others can find ideas within the thesis that are worthy of one or two articles.

Many people, however, experience discomfort at the thought of revisiting their final project from graduate school. They spent so much time and effort on this work that even thinking about it again can be depressing. For these people it is probably better to leave the thesis behind and all its bittersweet memories. The experience of one of our colleagues illustrates some of the possible frustrations. She repackaged her thesis into several articles and received back rejections with comments like, "This reads like a doctoral thesis." She realized that her heart was no longer in this work and she turned to another topic that she found more interesting; here she found success. Susan tried to repackage a part of her doctoral dissertation and when she submitted it for publication was told, "This is frankly boring." She had to agree with the reviews; she had been bored writing it, and it was a boring piece of work!

Glen agrees that many recent graduates are so tired with their graduate research that it is probably a good idea to put it away for a year and move on to new topics. On the other hand, it is important not to waste all of the time and energy that went into researching and writing the dissertation. It is probably a good idea to read the dissertation again at a later time and determine whether and how it might be published. Glen published a chapter of his dissertation as a journal article about two years after he graduated and he continues to use a number of the ideas he worked with during his graduate student days.

Working on a Collaborative Project

Where else can we look for interesting topics? One way is to work on someone else's already established project. Usually this means that someone on faculty has a research grant and needs extra hands, or it may be someone with a great idea who wants company in the research process. This can represent an opportunity to learn new research skills, to gain experience in academic writing with the guidance of a more senior colleague, or to develop an important mentor/protege relationship. This sort of relationship, however, can also be entrapping. A ready made project does not require the creative spirit necessary for generating one's own project, and it will require hours and hours of work that can be grinding when one is not intrinsically curious about the research under question. The caution here would be not to work on a project unless it excites you intellectually. Writing without this lens can be a deadly and exhausting process which may lead to getting published, but often leaves little love for the process.

The experience of one graduate student speaks candidly to the issue of writing only to get published. She found herself in a course where, unexpectedly, the final product was to submit a paper for publication. In reflecting on this process she wrote:

> I had a terrible time trying to come up with a subject I felt passionate about. I finally came up with one that I felt was at least current and proceeded to write the paper. It was a long and painful process. I submitted my paper with little or no confidence that it would ever be published. Low and behold, three months later I received a letter of acceptance. At first I was in shock, then excited and then uncomfortable. I wrote that paper because I had to–not because I felt strongly about the topic. Wouldn't this have shown in the writing? How could they publish something I was not committed to and felt no real connection with? Should I now try and make it my cause? I have not been able to come to terms with this dilemma. I was not connected to my true beliefs. It has made me realize that writing a paper for the sake of a mark is as disconnected from learning as you can get. I look upon the publication of my paper with dread.

Action Research

Surely there has to be some formula that will lead to compelling ideas worth exploring in a written context? Action research on one's own pedagogy can lead the academic to rich possibilities. What are you doing as an academic that is different? Do you teach differently? Assess differently? How do your students experience your classes? Is your department involved in an unique professional development experience? All around us there is fruitful material for the writer. A good starting point is looking at where you spend the most energy. For example, one of our colleagues was finding it hard to find a "special" topic that was interesting enough to her that she could justify spending time on it. Meanwhile, she was taking a leadership role in her faculty and facilitating the implementation of innovative programming. She realized that her real interests lay in this implementation. She began to take field notes of her own experiences and gathered other documentation during the implementation stages. This took her to the literature on organizational change. Suddenly she was researching what she most needed to know in a real life context. She abandoned the many half hearted efforts that she had started, but hadn't been able to motivate herself to finish. Now her writing has real meaning and purpose for her and this is reflected in the quality of her recent writing efforts.

Documenting your own teaching strategies can also be a fertile field for publication. Most disciplines seems to have journals devoted to the act of teaching and/or professional development. Higher education journals explore the dynamics of what is happening at college and university levels. Susan is very interested in innovative teaching strategies. As she experiments with alternative teaching strategies at the higher education level she also treats the process as a formal research process. In this way she is killing two birds with one stone and insures that she is always interested in both what she is doing and what she is writing.

Book Reviews

Book reviews are often recommended as an easy way to get started in the writing process. In our experience, there can be some pitfalls with this. One, many journals only accept solicited book reviews. This is not always made clear on the instructions to contributors. It is a good idea to check with a journal first before sending off an unsolicited review. Two, journals sometimes specialize in different sorts of reviews. Some only carry long critical reviews, others want a brief overview of the book and some indication of the audience that would find it useful. Again you need to be clear on the required approach. Finally, books take a long time to read. When you are reviewing a book you have to read it very carefully in order to do it justice. Make sure if you go this route that the book merits the attention that you will have to give it and that you will enjoy reading it. If it is an essential book for your own understanding of a topic then reviewing it means meeting dual objectives at the same time.

Books

When Glen was interviewed for an academic position at a large university he asked one of the administrators to describe the level of publication considered appropriate for someone applying for tenure. He was told that a new professor who published three peer reviewed journal articles each year should have no difficulty. Less would be required if the scholar is responsible for ground breaking work that represents a major contribution to the field.

When Glen asked about books the administrator paused for a long, long time. "When it comes to new faculty and tenure," the individual finally responded, "books can be very, very risky."

The answer to these questions will vary by field of study, for example biology versus history, and by institution. Glen has received quite different answers from officials at different universities. It is a very good idea to consult with your colleagues and academic administrators as you begin to plan your career in academic writing.

This is especially important if you are considering writing or editing a book since this can be a somewhat riskier starting place for new writers than some of the other types of projects we have described above. There are two types of risks involved: the tremendous amount of time and energy required to complete a book project, and the way in which the book will be viewed by other scholars.

Writing a book often takes a long time and requires a great deal of dedication. There is no question that the end result can be tremendously satisfying both in personal and professional terms, but those rewards can be a long time in coming since there is so much more work and many steps involved in writing a large manuscript compared with a number of smaller articles. The issue is whether a book is the best way to start your writing career. If you have more to say than can be contained in a single journal article or you want to publish the results of a large study, then a book may well be the most appropriate medium for your work. On the other hand, you may be able to learn more about yourself and your writing process by starting with a series of smaller projects and building up your knowledge, experience, and confidence to a point where a book becomes the next logical step in an evolving career. Developing a track record in journal articles will also assist in establishing your academic reputation in your chosen field, and that reputation will make it easier for you to sell your book idea.

Writing the leading book in an academic field can have a very positive influence on your career, but if a book written by a new scholar is very poorly received, and if this book was the only piece of writing that the individual has to show for the "publish or perish" review of tenure, the situtation can be quite uncomfortable. This is the other type of risk associated with writing a book–of counting on a book to bring success and then finding that it was easier to find someone to publish the book than it was to get other academics to like it. This is another good reason to establish your reputation as an academic writer first, and then setting your sights on a book at a point in your career when you are more professionally secure and have a clearer sense of hoow your work fits in. We do not want to discourage you from writing a book, but we do think that you shouldd be aware of the risks involved.

You will find a number of very good reference works on the process of writing and submitting book projects, as well as lists of book publishers by field of interest, in your local library, and we strongly encourage you to do research on the "nuts and bolts" of book publishing before your project.

- What doea a book proposal look like?
- What are the three or four most reputable publishers in your field of study?
- Is there a series editor that you can talk to about your ideas?
- What does a book contract look like?
- Will the book be peer reviewed and will the publication be regarded as a major contribution when it comes time for your tenure review?
- Do you have professional colleagues who can offer you adive?

As a final note on writing and editing books, think about how you can combine projects in order to meet several professional objectives at the same time. Perhaps that huge volume of notes that you keep refining for your favourite course could become a seminal textbook. Many edited books are based on the contributions to a thematic academic conference. Why not organize a conference on a topic that you find particularly stimulating? If there are very good papers presented at the conference (which will probably be the case since you will have invited many of the top names in the field–a good opportunity to increase your network of contacts as well as your reputation), perhaps an edited book or a special issue of an academic journal would be a natural next step. Also, instead of writing a book from scratch, why not start by publishing a series of articles and then consider combining or organizing these ideas in the form of a book.

Finding your own voice in academic publishing not only means finding what you really want to say about topics and issues that stimulate you, it also means finding your own way in terms of getting your ideas into print. There are a range of options available, but there is no one approach that is right for everyone, in the same way that there is no single right way to build other aspects of your academic career. You must do what seems right to you. For some, that means a very strategic approach where every step in the development of their career is mapped out in advance. For others, it means doing what feels right without a clear sense oof a master plan. You can follow any one (or two or three) of thousands of paths to success; the only thing we strongly suggest is that you make sure that you make it your own path, after all it is your career, and that you are aware that there are other ways you could go.

Finding the Right Journal

IN EXPLORING DIFFERENT approaches to writing, you may have noticed that we occasionally referred to the journal targeted for publication. Choosing a focus and finding the right journal are inextricably linked. This is because different journals have different perspectives and publish different types of articles. We both agree that finding the right journal is crucial to success in getting published. It also will lessen the possibility of rejection. Both of us have developed strategies to finding the right journal.

Creating a Personalized Data Base

Each of us has found different routes to systematically organizing our efforts toward publishing. Susan bought a large binder and labelled it "Publication Possibilities." She was ready to create her own data base and spent many hours in the library leafing through journals. Sometimes she resented this time that she could have spent writing–but realized later how essential this step was. When she found a journal, she would look over the table of contents and skim through the journal to see the type of articles it published. Since most of Susan's work is qualitative research, she would eliminate journals where each article displayed pages of charts with statistical results. When she found a good fit, she would then proceed to photocopy the appropriate pages for her personalized filing system. During this process, she discovered that there were a vast number of journals and that there were many possible places where she could send her material. Now she continues to add to her collection. An added bonus is finding interesting articles that contribute to her research!

Glen finds it helpful to keep extensive background files on each writing project. He keeps all of his correspondence with editors, his notes on different journal possibilities, and all of his research material organized in binders or files corresponding to the title of the final paper. When he is considering a new project he will often return to these files for hints on how the new paper might be treated by the journal and tries to learn from his prior successes and problems. Sometimes a reviewer's critique of an old article suggests an idea for a new piece.

A particularly important factor for Glen is to get a sense of a journal's readership. Writing for an international audience may mean that you will have to provide background information that would be unnecessary in a journal directed towards American or Canadian readers. He has also found that some American journals are not very interested in articles that describe the Canadian experience and vice versa. These are things he looks for when he encounters a new journal and that he notes in his data base.

Over the years you can develop a pretty informative personalized data base of possible places to publish. Coming from a small university we have found it very helpful to visit the university libraries from larger centres. Here we can skim through journals that are not available at our home institution. As well, when we read through the literature we often find references to journals that sound interesting. This alerts us to look for these journals.

When a new editor takes over a journal he or she sometimes decides to shift the direction or focus of the publication. These sorts of announcements are often made in a special journal editorial. Reading these announcements can sometimes provide hints on what sorts of "new" material the editor is now looking for, or suggest that a journal that has been dominated by one particular approach or style is actively seeking work of another form. These announcements can play a special role in your data base.

One pitfall to creating your own data base is the possibility that it becomes outdated. For this reason Susan often skims through her *Publication Possibilities* binder looking for possible places to send a certain article. Once she has narrowed down the field she reviews a current issue of a selected journal to ensure that it has the same editor, same address and same instructions to contributors. If the journal is not readily available, a quick phone call will give you the same information and save you the expense of sending multiple copies of an article to the wrong address.

Other Avenues

In Susan's field there is a book called *Cabell's Directory of Publishing Opportunities in Education* where over 500 current journals are summarized and the reader is informed of editorial emphasis, review process, acceptance rate, type of reader the journal attracts and the time required for review. It also offers the instructions to the contributors. As well, the *Phi Delta Kappan* often offers an update on useful information for many journals such as: percentages of articles accepted, percentage of solicited articles, number of readers, refereed or non refereed, number of reviewers. This kind of overview helps to avoid sending articles to journals that only accept solicited articles or ones that always have a theme issue. Similar resources are available in business and economics, engineering, health sciences and medicine, history, languages and literature, law, library and information science, philosophy, political science, psychology, social sciences, and social work (Luey, 1990).

One piece of useful advice is that you have a greater possibility for success if you write for a theme issue (provided you have a genuine interest in the theme and something fresh to say). Thus, it makes good sense to keep an eye out for a call for papers that are in your area. In addition to special notices in the journal, these announcements are sometimes published in the *Chronicle of Higher Education* (United States), the *Times Higher Education Supplement* (United Kingdom), and *University Affairs* (Canada).

These avenues offer a short cut to creating your own data base, but there is still something to be said for having seen a copy of a journal in order to get a real feel for its perspective. For us, these materials offer a useful extension to our own personalized systems. However, if you can't find such a resource in your own field, here is a perfect opportunity for you to be the creator of such a text!

Many large research conferences hold regular sessions on how to get published. There are usually presentations by the editors of various journals. These presentations offer good advice on exactly what a journal is looking for and can save many hours of searching. As well, successful authors sometimes speak about the secrets to their success which can be very illuminating.

Susan recently attended a panel discussion on how to get

published. Much of the session was delivered by editors who talked about editorial secrets–each journal valuing different topics and approaches to writing. Finally, three successful authors offered their advice by telling their own stories. It was clear that each one had followed their own path and written what they truly believed in and felt was important. She was also struck by how "entrepreneurial" each speaker had been. They had called up editors to run by new ideas and two of them had made special efforts to take an editor out for breakfast in order to "sell" their ideas. As someone intimidated by editors, she was quite astonished by this approach. It made her realize that editors are human and approachable–although she has yet to take such a bold step.

Like Susan, Glen has been reluctant to directly approach editors to discuss new projects, but a number of his writing projects have been commissioned by individuals editing books or reference works. These have usually been individuals he has met at conferences or had informal contact with via the mail. The more you write and contribute to scholarly discussions the more opportunities will come your way.

Rule of Three

One of the most practical pieces of publishing advice Susan has heard is the "rule of three." According to this rule you select three journals where your article could possibly fit before you even start writing. Then, if the first attempt is rejected, you send the article out immediately to another journal and finally to a third, if necessary. This is done without revision–unless you are given some sage advice in the review process that is easy to address. This "rule of three" guarantees that you have a number of papers in circulation and somehow makes the sting of rejection easier. If the article doesn't attract any of three journals, it may need serious revisions or may even need to be scrapped.

Although Susan has learned to write for a particular journal she has found it hard to follow the "three" rule. As a result she has one or two papers that still sit on her shelf after a particularly vicious rejection. She knows that this is rather silly since she has personally experienced being "third time lucky." Rejections are not necessarily based on a lack of quality as much as a lack of right fit. Keep trying and you probably will eventually find that fit!

Many of our colleagues talk this rule, but don't actually practice it. In spite of their best intentions they find themselves writing an article without a specific audience and then scrambling for a journal at the end. Although some have success with this approach, we have seen too many casualties along the way and would encourage you to take the time and discipline to tailor your writing to a specific journal. Writing with a particular journal and audience in mind will help you make decisions about style, format and language. It will also save you time later since you will have already followed the style and writing guidelines associated with your first choice journal.

Dealing with Rejection

Unfortunately, a very real risk in sending out material for publication is the possibility of it being rejected. Rejection is part of the process and all successful writers will be able to tell stories of rejection slips. Generally the advice is to expect a certain amount of rejection but do not take it personally. As a graduate student, Susan heard that finding the right journal was key to publication success. However, she wasn't quite sure what that meant. The common advice was to begin with low profile, non refereed Canadian publications. This would offer a stepping stone to higher profile publications. This advice, although well meaning, made little sense to her. Susan believed that she had something to say and, since there were ample journals, she reasoned she would have just as much luck with the more prestigious journals as with the more local ones. At grad school, this talk on how to get published was only idle chatter. She moved on to a one year contract position. In mid year, she suddenly had the opportunity to apply for a tenure track position. She was warned that the job was highly competitive and that, at the very least, she had to have several articles that were being considered for publication. In an unprecedented burst of energy (motivated by the sheer terror of not having any job) she pulled together seven journal articles and sent them off to the heavy weight refereed journals. At the time of the interview process, seven articles were out for review. Fortunately, she had already published a co authored book and two articles which strengthened her application.

Susan got the job, but six out of seven of her articles were rejected. Six rejections offered a clear message, and Susan, devastated, wondered if she would ever get published. Could she write? Did she have anything to say? Then she focused on the advice she had been given. Had she sent each paper to the *right* journal? As she thought about this, Susan realized that she had done little research on these journals. Did the journals publish articles with topics similar to hers? Was the writing style similar? At this point she became more "scientific" about the process. Once she did additional research on the "right journal," each of the articles found a home–and not in the low profile publications once suggested by her "mentors."

One of the first articles Glen worked on was a co authored paper based on a small research project. After finishing the first draft he circulated the paper to a number of individuals he respected and asked for feedback. The feedback he received was kind but almost totally negative. He put the paper away for a few weeks and then read it again. It occurred to him that one of the possible problems with the paper was the way in which he had framed the study (what media consultants sometimes refer to as the "spin"). He rewrote the opening and closing sections of the paper, essentially placing the study in a different context, and then recirculated the paper. The response was completely different this time, and several of the readers actually thought that Glen and his co author had redone the study.

Publishing the paper turned out to be the next challenge. Six months later the paper had been rejected by two journals and Glen began to seriously wonder whether the study was "good enough" for scholarly publication. By this time, however, Glen believed that he had a large amount of time and energy invested in the paper and he really did not see any harm in continuing the submission process. It was the right decision, and the third journal accepted the paper for publication without revisions.

Writing Your Way To Clarity

WHEN SUSAN ATTENDED a conference presentation on how to get published, the advice of one successful author rang particularly true to her. He talked about writing around a body of ideas rather than about a specific topic. He told stories of years of writing about his ideas for good pedagogy that were not absolutely clear to him, but that he was convinced were important. These ideas were not immediately well received, but he continued to write. He also sent out his work to as many people as possible for feedback. Although few offered any comments, he found that the ones that did helped to further clarify his own thoughts–and one who responded was a prestigious publisher who, years later, published many of his books.

In part, this author's tenacity came from his deep belief in his ideas. He recommended that others write about ideas and not worry if they are not absolutely clear at first. The ideas will eventually crystallize through the writing process itself. The important thing is to write and to seek out as much feedback as possible.

This takes us back to the problem of finding the right topic. We believe that we need to write about what is important to us. Hopefully, we can find something we feel passionate enough about that we are convinced it is worth expressing those ideas to others.

Still, this all sounds like serendipity. Often being trained in academia leaves people without a personal passion. Rather, we have been inundated with other academics as the experts and have been taught *not* to trust our own experiences. Books such as *Women's Way of Knowing* (Belenky, Clinchy, Goldberger, & Tarule, 1986) have opened up new avenues for academics. They identified objective, rational, procedural knowing as the only type of knowledge that is legitimized in academia. Their work identified subjective, intuitive knowing. For them the most sophisticated knowing involved connecting procedural knowing with the subjective, intuitive knowing to construct one's own meaning rather than relying on experts. The legitimization of this way of knowing allows the academic to explore new territory. We are the experts of our own experience and all have a certain amount of "experienced wisdom" to draw upon. What insights have we gained from our experiences? What do our subjective experiences tell us about the "knowledge" that we teach and the research that we conduct? How can these insights inform others? Try these ideas out through both teaching and writing. The writing part of this process we call "writing your way to clarity."

Writing your way to clarity means we begin the writing now–from where we are now. The assumption is that the ideas are not clear cut yet–rather the germs of ideas are seeds that will grow with care and cultivation. Understanding this concept, that the writing itself will help to clarify ideas, tends to lessen the frustration. And once a writer has experienced the increasing clarity it is easier to trust the process.

On Being Clear and Accessible

BOTH SUSAN AND GLEN BELIEVE that writing should be clear and accessible to the reader. Not all academics agree with this premise. Some prefer to write in a dense, jargon laden style. In conversation with such authors they often explain their approach by saying that their text challenges the reader to think in new ways. One cannot get through their writing without a great deal of effort–unless you are well versed in their field and the general tone of the ideas being put forth.

Susan writes about curriculum innovations and she wants people to be able to grasp these ideas with enough ease that they can apply them to current practice. As well, she appreciates reading new ideas that are written in a clear, concise fashion. She has struggled with the denser work of some of her colleagues and can appreciate their argument of the necessity to stretch one's thinking into new territories. For her, the struggle should be with the application of her ideas, not with deconstructing the text. Clearly these are personal choices that align with personal objectives. However, she does not believe that the presentation of a dense and difficult text should be a disguise for poor writing.

Given her preference for clear and articulate writing, Susan finds there are two good ways to clarify her ideas. The first is obviously to write–and rewrite–until a concept becomes clarified both on paper and in her own mind. During this writing she is addressing an imaginary audience. Secondly, she discusses her ideas with a very real audience, her students. For Susan, the classroom has offered a litmus test for the relevance of her ideas. She asks students to get involved in some experiential exercises that apply the ideas she is working on. This is how she learns about how people construct meaning from her ideas, which helps her to further clarify concepts and ensures that what she is writing about has authenticity. It also guarantees a dialectic between theory and practice.

Glen believes that the writing process is all about communication. The challenge in good writing is to find a way to communicate ideas to the audience, and this is sometimes more difficult than creating or developing your ideas in the first place.

Since he wants his contributions to be accessible to a wide audience, he will often experiment with different ways of communicating his ideas; sometimes spending hours playing with words and phrases until he is satisfied that he has found a good way of communicating a particular idea or notion. Since Glen enjoys playing with words, he knows that one of his potential problems is emphasizing form over content. When he has finished a draft of a paper he will put it aside for awhile. When he reads it again he will look for "favored phrases," expressions that might have given him particular pleasure in writing but which may actually detract from the basic communication of ideas.

While Glen and Susan approach writing in different ways, they both agree that the final product must represent their own voice. They differ in terms of how they try to find this voice, but they clearly agree that the challenge of good writing is to express one's own ideas in a clear, accessible way.

Getting Started

MUCH OF THE PROCESS HAS been outlined already. Begin with yourself and your practice and beliefs. Begin by writing, even if you aren't clear yet about what you want to say. The important part is to begin. There is differing advice on how to motivate oneself. Natalie Goldberg (1986, 1993) advocates a free flowing, but disciplined approach. She writes daily about the world around her from a Buddhist perspective. She describes writing with the flow, writing in a free flowing fashion about the world around us. For her, the key is in the writing process itself. She sits down to write on a regular basis. She writes on any topic that comes to mind, which may be her big toe or the chicken soup she had for lunch. This spontaneous writing helps get one started.

Robert Boice (1990) offers a self disciplined approach to the writer unable to schedule large blocks of time. He recommends that the academic schedule 30 minutes of writing into every work day. This must be 30 minutes of uninterrupted time; Boice offers several strategies to ensure lack of interruptions. This program even offers ways to motivate oneself through writer's block. If you do *not* write during certain periods you must commit $25.00 to your least favorite charity! Presumably the thought of doing this is so repugnant that it is better to write than not to.

For many, scheduling large blocks of time simply doesn't work. There is too much to do–classes to teach, committee meetings to attend, papers to grade, or personal agendas to complete. Since many of these other activities have specific deadlines, one may be tempted to avoid writing or to give it a lower priority. The challenge, it seems to us, is to find your own techniques for ensuring that you can find the time to write while also fulfilling your other responsibilities. We do not believe that there is a universal approach or a secret trick that will satisfy everyone–once again, it is a matter of finding your own way.

Glen finds that he cannot write every day. While he tries to think about his writing projects on a daily basis, he knows that his creative energies come in bursts and cycles. He finds that some of his best writing ideas come from long walks or conversations with colleagues, and he tries to find ways of storing these ideas for when he is in the right mood for writing. He also finds that he does not have the self control to write on a regular basis without creating artificial timelines for output. One of the reasons he sends paper proposals to scholarly conferences is because he knows that the deadlines established for the conference will provide him with the incentive and motivation necessary to finish the paper. Conference presentations effectively force him to write a solid first draft of a paper, and almost all of his conference papers are sent off to journals immediately after the conference.

Susan also finds that she needs blocks of time to write effectively. For example, this monograph was put on hold for two months because she needed several days with several hours to be able to fully move into her task. Then Glen got caught in a turmoil of deadlines and the project again was put on hold. The problem with this approach is that it can lead to self imposed guilt. However, we have come to enjoy writing enough to know that we will complete the task and schedule the needed blocks of time.

It seems to us that the answer to how to schedule time for writing, like all other answers to the writing process, lies within. Which way do you work better? Boice's approach has offered a successful writing path for many. Susan has tried the thirty minute blocks but she has not been good at deflecting interruptions and she found her own particular style of writing often could not be turned on and off in time slots. However, she has found enforced, 30 minute time slots a good answer for moving through endless paperwork that requires attention but little creativity.

There are other strategies that can motivate you to getting started. As previously mentioned, one excellent area for writing is to explore what and how one goes about the process of being an academic. How do you teach? What are you doing that is innovative and facilitates the desired learning outcomes? Every field has journals that publish articles on the teaching process itself. Data can be generated by keeping field notes or a journal of experiences. These projects are writing activities and can be considered part of writing the way to clarity. In this way, the author/teacher will be encouraged to reflect on teaching practices as well as theory.

Susan finds that many of her articles are about strategies she is using in the higher education classroom. Perhaps the riskiest example of this was a paper presented at an academic conference (Drake & Boak, 1992) of team teaching an educational research course. Susan was an untenured professor who held a strong commitment to qualitative methodology; she was working with her Dean who espoused an integrative approach that included a heavy emphasis on the quantitative. As part of the course structure, students were asked to keep field notes of the classes, develop a research question, and write a case study about the experience. Susan and the Dean also wrote field notes. The 18 case studies prepared by the students shed a new light on what we, the professors, "thought" we had been teaching and forced us both to re examine our basic beliefs about teaching and learning. This paper is in the process of being published as a chapter in a forthcoming book.

Sharing with colleagues offers another route to polishing ideas. This works particularly well if there is a small network of people who are interested in your field and committed to collegial relationships. This needs to be a reciprocal arrangement or colleagues tend to feel abused and offer little satisfactory feedback. In one university, a small group of women have joined together formally to create the Centre on Collaborative Research. They volunteer to peer review each other's work. As well, they deliberately send out conference proposals and then apply subtle pressure on each other to make certain that these presentations become publications. This arrangement seems to work well for them since there is both pressure and support being offered.

Exploring the Literature

WE BOTH AGREE THAT, as researcher and writers, we need to start by having some general idea of how an area of interest has been approached in the literature. However, we see this initial exploration somewhat differently. What exactly is the role of the review of the literature? For Susan, the assumption is that every academic has some working knowledge of their field of interest (although some of the most original and interesting ideas come from those who have not been previously immersed in the existing literature). Setting aside this general knowledge, Susan believes the next step is to sort out exactly what it is that you truly believe–based on personal experiences and *not* the accumulated evidence of "experts." In this way you can begin to bring fresh eyes to a set of ideas. You are not just repeating what is already out there. Part of the trick is to find a flaw in the implicit assumptions of the acknowledged experts. Is there a fresh twist on an old dilemma? This can lead to new experiments or conceptual frameworks that then need to be played out.

For Susan an intensive review of the literature comes last. There is a great deal of literature in our vast information highway. In doing literature reviews for a wide variety of eclectic topics, Susan has found that the prospective writer can find support for virtually any perspective on a topic. This particular approach of starting with your own ideas and then supporting them with existing research ensures that the academic writer begins with his or her own insights rather than the thoughts of others. Susan has found this to be a guaranteed route to both finding your voice and assuring that you have fresh insights to add to your particular field.

Glen sees the initial review of the literature differently. He likes to view his writing as part of a dialogue with the scholarly literature in his field. While he begins with a personal topic or question he wants to explore, he then likes to review how others have looked at the subject. How can he locate his ideas within the research literature on the topic? What can other scholars tell him about the subject, or about how he might approach the subject? How can he contribute something new to this academic discussion?

He begins with these questions because he believes that he can learn from participating in this form of intellectual dialogue with other scholars. If he proceeds too far in his writing without first reviewing the literature, he may find that he is simply duplicating work that someone has already done, instead of furthering the scholarly conversation. The challenge he sets for himself is to find a way of contributing something new to this ongoing dialogue. For him a close connection to the literature is essential from the beginning.

Regardless of how you first approach the literature, we would like to offer some strategies that helped us through long hours in the library.

Data Bases

In the world of academia there are vast numbers of journals that exist and a variety of topics that they cover. A first step to any major review should be an exploration of relevant data bases. Given the information highway, the nature of the library is under transformation. A great deal of information is available through electronic media. As a result, academics who have access to a computer have access to a bewildering array of choices and information. Deciding on what is important to read becomes a real skill. Many articles can be found through indexes and bibliographies in the new electronic library system. This makes it important to know the key words in your subject area in order to narrow down the field. If you don't have luck with one set of key words, try another. Although it is easy to assume that there is no literature in your topic–there seems to be literature on everything–we just may not have found it!

It seems almost essential to be connected to Internet. This way you have automatic access to the great library systems of the world. Before starting a search, check with the librarian for current innovations to help you. For example, there is software available that will allow you to peruse the table of contents of selected journals of your choice. When you see the title of an article that may be of interest, you can ask for the abstract. All of this can be done before you even set foot in the library.

When Susan was first writing her dissertation on imagery she couldn't find many citations in any data base. By "snowballing" the literature she found the use of imagery tucked within articles on many diverse topics. Three years later when revisiting the topic, the data base had grown from 35 entries to well over 300. These included some of the articles she had discovered in her original search, but that had not been included in the data base. The reason? The librarian reported that the key words were not recognized in the original search three years before, but were now identified as important concepts. This experience taught her not to rely fully on computer searches. As well, she found that the abstracts in the data bases can be misleading. After actually reading the paper, quite different information may emerge. If you want to actually cite a reference it is extremely important to take the time to read.

Snowball Approach

Another particularly profitable way to review relevant literature is the "snowball" approach. Armed with your area of interest, go to the journal stacks and browse through several current journals. You will almost always find something that is relevant and current. Referring to the reference list of that article can lead you to other relevant material. This method can have surprising results.

Although the snowball technique sounds somewhat non systematic, it actually can be very profitable. When we hear of other researchers following this path, they usually express delight and surprise at how successful they can be at this seemingly "intuitive" system. Finding even two or three articles will lead you to other articles and ultimately reveal the seminal works that are so important to include in any literature review. Backed up by a computer search, you should be able to develop a sound literature base. The one drawback of this system is that you need to find a very recent article so that its review of the literature is current.

Reviewing Systematically

How do you systematically collect data for the literature review? It is very easy to become overwhelmed with lots of little pieces of paper with scraps of information on them. There are several systems for organization that can help. The traditional method is to use index cards to record pertinent information on a topic. The cards then can be filed in a filing box and referred to easily. This system does work, although it takes the discipline of carefully selecting relevant material and copying it down. We would suggest writing down exact quotations that you might use. Be sure to include quotation marks and page numbers. Another advantage of this system is that you can highlight the cards for particularly useful information and you can shuffle them easily to reconstruct the theoretical position you may be espousing.

Some people prefer to photocopy pertinent articles and file them for future use. However, this is a very expensive way to collect the literature and many of the papers go unread. As well, they quickly tend to be out of date. We recommend only photocopying the key articles that are central to your topic. These then can be filed in large manila folders under the topic heading for quick and easy reference.

One of the most frustrating aspects of writing is not having accurate citations at your finger tips. This frustration can be eliminated with a little disciplined organization. If you have access to the library system through an electronic data base, much of the information needed on a reference list is available to you readily. However, there were many evenings during the completion of her doctoral thesis that Susan found herself trudging to the library to look for some missing piece of information in her bibliography. Most often she was missing the page numbers for a chapter in an edited book. Experiences like these have taught us to be disciplined enough to write down the complete reference each time we are exploring a piece of literature.

Since many of the journals in our fields request the use of style guidelines prescribed by the American Psychological Association, we copy citations using this style. However, we have also learned to include the full name of the author and the month as well as the volume of any journal we are using. Too often we have been caught with having to switch from APA to Chicago style and suddenly need first names and months rather than volume numbers. Check to see that you have the page numbers for the book chapters you are citing, and make certain that all the pertinent information is available on the photocopies you make. It is surprising how often one small, but necessary, detail is missing. This often feels like tedious work, but work you will be glad to endure after too many trips to the library to fill in the blanks you have missed.

If you follow these steps when considering the literature you find some of the major frustrations are lessened. Knowing the journals that you are writing for makes the task easier. However, if you follow the rule of thumb of sending your article out to three journals before significant revisions, you may need to revise the reference list according to the specification of the alternative journals. This method allows you to move from journal to journal with relative ease.

Reviewing With the Computer

Many of the problems just mentioned can be easily eliminated by entering the literature review on a computer program. You can call up key words yourself and the computer will shuffle the information you have put in. This approach is wonderful if you are computer literate.

Glen uses a bibliographic program for compiling reference lists and keeping notes, and another program to help him organize ideas for large projects. If you feel comfortable with using a computer, you may wish to invest in software for reasons other than simply word processing. Notebook computers also allow you to write and take notes where ever you want to work: the coffee shop, in your back yard with a glass of wine, or in the library. However, do not forget that the computer is an expensive tool, and one that can be prone to theft if left unattended.

Organizing for Clarity

THIS SECTION IS NOT INTENDED to be a stylistic primer. The stand that we have taken in our own writing is that we want our work to be accessible to the reader. This means clean, well written sentences that display an absence of jargon. There are, however, many small techniques that can help the writer to be clear and therefore more easily understood. It is always handy to have a classic guide such as Strunk and White (1979) or the style manual most often used in your field when questions of style emerge. In our field we tend to use the *Chicago Manual of Style* (1982) or the American Psychological Association manual (1994). As well, most word processing programs include a grammar check. Having the patience to go through a grammar check is usually worth the effort. Many academics complain that the only consistent message they get is, "you may be using the passive voice." The active voice does have more power and you will probably also find other mistakes that somehow slipped into the manuscript.

Our assumption is that today's writers are using a computer. If you are not, it is almost a compulsory investment. Sharing a secretary with many other academics can cut your productivity in half. With a computer you can quickly edit your own papers and be in control of administrative details.

The computer can be the main vehicle toward easing the pain of writing. However, if you don't type with ease (as is the case for Susan who taught herself with a computer program), it does take time to conquer keyboarding and to learn to write in a new way. Working with a word processing program seems to demand a new way of thinking and expressing oneself. The flow is different. Susan finds that when she has been away from writing for awhile her first couple of paragraphs are uncomfortable and disjointed. She has come to understand that she needs to work and rework ideas before really getting started. This is writing her way to clarity. Her thinking processes and keyboarding fingers are warming up. However, once you get over the initial hurdles, writing with the computer can be a very creative process.

Susan is writing her part of this monograph in long hand. This is largely because Glen uses a different computer program. The style of her writing is much different than if she were working on the computer. There is no space for making adjustments, for shifting one thought to another place in the document. The product is different. In this case, for example, she is writing something at this moment that is totally unplanned and may or may not fit the final flow of the document. Sometimes, this type of writing is preferable. Again this is a question to be answered by your inner wisdom.

Clarity of Purpose

One of the simplest rules for clarity is to be clear about the intentions of the research. First, the purpose of your study should be stated in the first two or three paragraphs. It is very easy to get lost in words, building up an argument for writing your paper at all. However, the reader needs to know right away what he or she will be reading. This tendency to leave the main intent of the study until well into the paper is a fairly wide spread tendency within academia. Susan only discovered it after many reviewers commented that it was a personal flaw in her own writing. Then, as a reviewer, she began to identify this problem with many other writers. Now she forces herself to clearly state the main goal of the paper in the first paragraph or two. Often this runs against her personal desire to create a powerful setting for the story she is going to tell. In fact, even as she was writing this section, she had a paper returned for revision where she had left the key point of the article until the end. She was shocked at her own mistake because she definitely knew better! When she places herself in the reader's (or the reviewer's) shoes she sees how important this is.

As a graduate student, Susan's professor, Dr. Joel Weiss of the Ontario Institute for Studies in Education, taught her a formula for beginning a paper that she has found invaluable. It is a four step process: (1) stating the common assumption underlying most research in this area, (2) pointing out a possible flaw in this assumption, (3) stating the purpose of the study which will be a further study of the flaw in the initial assumption, (4) outlining the significance of the current study. Susan has found that when she can reduce her intention to four statements she is very clear, not only to herself, but also to her readers. This process then helps to clarify one's own thoughts as well as clarify the writing. Let's apply the formula to this monograph.

1. There are many books available that will guide the academic to fine academic writing.
2. Yet the act of writing remains difficult for a large majority of academics.
3. The purpose of this book is to explore the process of academic writing from a non traditional or non conventional lens based on an inside out approach successfully used in the field.
4. If other academics find some of the ideas in this monograph, useful, they may be motivated to write more and the academic field will be enriched.

The next step would be to flesh these four statements out by including the literature. You may recognize the following from the introduction of this book:

> There are many books available that will guide the academic to substantive academic writing (Simon, 1994; Moxley, 1992; Boice, 1990; Luey, 1990.) However, according to Robert Boice, a well known authority on writing, approximately 85% of publications are written by 15% of the academic population. Academics experience the writing process as very difficult and painful. As a result they give up writing rather than try to surmount the obstacles. This monograph takes a fresh look at the publishing game and offers tried and true strategies that allowed two new academics to experience publishing success. It is hoped that by offering these strategies other academics may reframe and refocus their writing endeavors to facilitate more ease in the writing process and therefore to experience greater success in academic publishing.

Departing from the tried and true may be a more authentic way for you to write but raises the chances of rejection. Timing is important when breaking from tradition. One year Susan and her colleagues presented a paper at the American Educational Research Association and were told by their discussants that their paper would not be discussed because they did not consider it to be research. As first time attendees of this conference they were horrified by this response to a study they considered to have involved rigorous research procedures.

They decided that the discussants had not understood their research because they had broken from tradition and used story as the medium to describe it. Trusting their own experiences, they reorganized the paper under more traditional headings and subsequently had the paper published in the *International Journal of Qualitative Research* (Drake, Elliott, & Castle, 1993). However, they have noticed that some ground breaking work has since appeared in the journal sponsored by the same organization where they made their disastrous "story" presentation. Other academics have moved out of the traditional mode into story to express authenticity in their work. These authors (Hollingsworth, 1992; Johnson, 1992) claim that their method of collaborative research calls for new ways of creating text and they have successfully challenged the traditional mode to do so. Had Susan and their colleagues presented their paper today, they may have had more success with their original approach at AERA. Again, timing is all.

At times, however, you may feel the absolute necessity of speaking in your own voice in your own way. To us, this is when you truly believe what you have to say is important and can only be said in a certain way. This rings true for both of us. Susan was working on mythology as a metaphor for personal transformation. Using the work of Joseph Campbell she found herself using words that could be considered non academic such as "path with heart." Although she was warned against this type of language, she knew intuitively that people could and did make sense of this. Eventually she found acceptance of these concepts in even mainstream arenas.

Glen sometimes finds that his work is criticized at conferences by individuals who work in related areas and who would like him to use their work as a way of framing the subject he is writing about. He is usually able to publish these papers without changes, and he has come to realize that all of his work has to stand or fall based on his own, and not someone else's understanding of the world. The moral of these stories is that we do have to follow our own "path with heart" in the publishing game. It is a hard call to make. Sometimes it is better to be heard in the more traditional mode than not to be heard at all.

Editing

Unfortunately few pieces of writing seem to come out perfectly the first time. We have come to accept that most of our writing will have to go through the editing process. Here is where working on a computer is so helpful. Taking a few days off from a particular piece allows us to return to our writing with fresh eyes. Then we can more fully appreciate if our sentences are grammatically correct and if there is a logical flow to the material. Trying to edit something is very hard when it is an ongoing process. It seems we get so locked into what we think we want to say, that we don't realize when we didn't say it effectively.

Incubation time is also helpful when one is going through the process of "writing your way to clarity." Taking a clean break seems to allow for thoughts to percolate in the consciousness. Treat yourself to a breath of fresh air, a leisurely walk around campus, or a one week holiday from writing on a particular project. Often, when we return to the text it seems to reorganize itself into a much more logical and/or meaningful manner. For many it is helpful to be working on two or three projects at the same time so that you can continue writing on another project while you incubate on the first one. An added bonus here is that often the ideas in your alternative projects interconnect and this enriches the incubation process.

Another shortcut in the editing process is to share your manuscript with a trusted colleague. This means choosing people who have your best interests at heart and who have *some* working knowledge of your topic. It also means that this will probably be a reciprocal arrangement. Constructive advice is often as close as the next office when we find the courage to share. The key is to find friends or colleagues that you trust; there is nothing gained from having your paper read by an individual whose opinions you will automatically discard.

One final suggestion about the editing process. We would recommend responding when a journal offers a critique and asks for substantial revisions. This is even if you are following the three journal rule suggested previously. In our experience we have found that the revisions are often sound and enrich the original work. As well, once revised the article stands an excellent chance of being selected. Although this often can be seen as too much work, it seems to be a more fruitful application of time than starting over with another journal. A bird almost in the hand is worth more than one in the bush.

Journal Editors and Editorial Boards

EVERY JOURNAL IS DIFFERENT. Each focuses on a particular area of knowledge, though in some cases this area has been rather broadly defined, and each has acquired an audience of individuals, organizations, and library patrons which share an interest in this area. However, it is important to recognize that journals not only differ in terms of what they publish, there are also important differences in how they decide what to publish and how they interact with potential contributors.

Peer reviewed journals play a very important role in the academic world. Peer review refers to the decision making process that the journal uses to determine the suitability of a submission for publication. The central notion in this process is that the best people to make judgments on an academic paper are individuals who are regarded as experts in the subject. The fact that these journals attempt to make decisions based on the evaluation of manuscripts by experts often means that they are accorded a higher status in the academic world than journals where all publication decisions are made by an editor or by editorial staff.

When you send a paper to a peer review journal the first person to read it will usually be the editor. The editor's job at this stage is to determine whether the paper matches the objectives and interests of the journal. A journal that focuses on the politics of South American countries will not be interested in a paper that involves an analysis of the writings of Virginia Woolf, even if it is the very best paper on that subject that has ever been written. If the editor doesn't believe that the subject of the paper matches the area of journal coverage, your paper will probably be returned to you.

The editor is also reading the paper with the idea of trying to identify individuals who might be called on to review it. Reviewers are usually individuals who have published articles on the same subject or a related issue. Since it is important for the editor to trust the judgment of the reviewers, most editors compile lists of individuals who have provided satisfactory feedback to the journal in the past. Reviewers who provide thoughtless, rather than thoughtful, criticism or who fail to comply with the deadlines prescribed by the editor are usually dropped from the list. The editor's job is to ensure that the reviewers have expertise in the topic of the paper, and this often means trying to identify new reviewers that the journal has not used before. One obvious place to look for the names of potential reviewers is in the list of citations you include in your paper. If you have based some of your ideas on the writings of Smith, it would not be at all unusual for the editor to ask Smith to review your paper.

Your paper will now be sent to at least two, and sometimes four or more reviewers. Each reviewer is asked to comment on the suitability of the manuscript for publication, sometimes using a form that has been developed by the journal.

These reviews are then returned to the editor who carefully reads the comments and makes one of three decisions concerning the manuscript. If all of the reviews are glowingly positive and there are few suggestions for changes, the editor will probably decide to publish the paper. If all of the reviewers are quite negative, the editor will probably decide not to publish. The third option is to ask the author to modify the paper to address the concerns of the reviewers. Since the editor has no way of knowing whether you are willing to modify the paper, or even if you can modify the paper to satisfy the reviewers, the editor cannot offer any guarantee of publication and you will receive a carefully worded letter.

It is very important to recognize that receiving a request for modifications or revisions from an editor is a very common experience. There is no such thing as the perfect academic paper. Reviewers and editors will sometimes identify points or ideas that should be clarified or suggest ways of improving how you present certain information. They may want you to think about concepts or ideas that you had not previously considered in the paper, or to delete elements of the paper that they believe distract the reader from your central idea. You and the editor share a common purpose; you both want to publish material that you will be proud of.

This last point is also important to remember when you

receive suggestions for revisions that don't seem right to you. Sometimes reviewers do not read the manuscript carefully enough or they simply disagree with the form or content of the paper. This may create a situation where a reviewer will ask for revisions that you feel are inappropriate or impossible. Glen has found that the best way to deal with this situation is to use those ideas that will assist in strengthening the paper. When he sends the revised paper back to the editor he includes a covering letter which details the changes that have been made and explains why he did not follow all of the suggestions made by the reviewers. While he finds that the paper is usually published, there are times when the author and the journal will disagree on the suitability of the paper, and this is when you simply submit the paper to the next journal on your list.

If the suggested revisions were relatively minor and you were able to address them all, the editor will probably decide to publish the manuscript. If major modifications were required, the editor may send the paper back to the original reviewers for feedback and the entire cycle will begin again.

Do the reviewers know who the author of the paper is? The answer to that question depends on the policies of the journal. Many journals use a double blind review process where the reviewers are not provided with the name of the author and the author is never informed of the names of the reviewers. This process is designed to create a high level of fairness through anonymity. Reviewers do not know whether the paper was written by the leading scholar in the field or a first time author. Since the author will not know who reviewed the paper, reviewers are free to comment as they please without fear of being verbally abused at the next academic conference by a disgruntled author. In a double blind review process, only the editor knows who wrote the paper and the names of the reviewers. Some journals use a one way blind review process where the names of the reviewers are held in confidence but reviewers are provided with the name of the author, some journals use an open process where there is no attempt to hide the identity of anyone involved, and others use a combination of approaches. Some journals use a double blind review process but allow reviewers to voluntarily identify themselves. Since this process involves human beings, problems can arise regardless of what policies are used, but many within the academic community believe that a double blind review holds the greatest potential for fairness and relative objectivity.

Most journals try to operate as efficiently as possible, but, since they often rely on the mail and the voluntary work of external reviewers, few journals can provide you with feedback in less than six or eight weeks, and many editors will warn you that the process can take six or more months. Why does it take so long? The central reason is that journals have created processes designed to ensure that their standards of quality are maintained. For example, Glen was a member of the editorial board of *Interchange*, an international journal which publishes papers on a wide range of topics related to education. All papers submitted to the journal are first read by the editor. Each paper is then read by two members of the editorial board who are asked to comment on the suitability of the paper for *Interchange*. The entire editorial board listens to the comments made by the two internal reviewers. If the paper is deemed to be suitable for the journal, it is then sent out for external review. Feedback from the external reviewers is discussed by the entire board before a decision concerning publication is made. All of the various steps in the peer review process take time.

Not all journals use peer review as a basis for making editorial decisions. In some cases the editor has full responsibility for making all decisions concerning manuscripts. Each paper is read by the editor and/or members of the editorial team and these individuals alone decide whether it is appropriate for publication. Since the journal does not use external readers for peer review, editorial decisions can be made relatively quickly.

As we have already noted, publishing an article in a peer reviewed journal usually carries more weight in academic circles than publishing an article in a journal that is not peer reviewed. This does not necessarily suggest that all peer reviewed journals are first rate, or that top quality papers are not published in editor controlled journals. There is a considerable range of quality associated with both types of journals.

When the journal decides to publish your paper the editor will write you a final letter. The editor will usually provide you with some indication of when the paper will appear in print. This time period can vary a great deal depending on the journal. The editor will also send you a formal document to sign concerning copyright, an indication of when you will be receiving galley proofs, and any other final instructions. Most journals ask that you assign almost all rights to the paper to the journal before publication. In other words, when the paper you wrote is finally published, the journal will own the rights to your paper. The document you will be signing is a formal legal contract and it is always wise to review the details to ensure that you agree with the prescribed terms.

One final point to keep in mind is that most scholarly journals are relatively small operations. Editors seldom receive much in the way of remuneration, and for many small journals the editor receives little more than the personal rewards associated with doing a good job and having a name on the inside cover of the publication. The fact that there are few staff means that some journals are forced to be extremely intolerant of papers that are poorly written or filled with grammatical errors. Some small journals don't even have the funds necessary to pay for a thorough copy edit of every paper that comes through. With this in mind, it is extremely important to make sure that your paper has very few grammatical or typographical errors–another reason to have a friend or colleague review it before you send the manuscript to a journal. If your paper is accepted by a journal you will be sent camera ready proofs, essentially an example of what your paper will look like in print. It is extremely important to review these proofs in detail. Glen once found that a typesetter had missed more than a paragraph of text and mangled several tables. Since some journals have little in the way of staff, they often rely on the author to ensure that the manuscript is ready for publication.

Patience is a virtue in journal publication. The process always takes longer than you think. On the other hand, there is nothing quite like the feeling of opening a letter from an editor and learning that your paper will be published.

Finally, a word about electronic journals. Over the last few years there has been a tremendous growth in the use of the Internet as a forum for the dissemination of research papers and information. Electronic journals are now operating in a wide variety of fields and there is little doubt that the number of these journals will increase in the next few years. New technologies (such as World Wide Web) will soon be employed to improve the visual quality of these journals, and there may well come a time when electronic journals achieve a high level of status in the academic world. However, most of these journals have had relatively little time to establish themselves within the academic community. While they represent an important new forum for disseminating your writing and certainly should not be ignored, it is important to consider the degree to which "publishing" in an electronic forum is respected in your field if you are concerned about tenure and promotion. Once again, do your homework before making a decision to send your magnum opus to a new journal.

Maintaining Self Motivation

How CAN WE MAINTAIN a satisfactory level of self motivation? In part, the process does this in itself. If you are writing your way to clarity you will find a certain sense of satisfaction as ideas take shape and fall into place. And once you begin to experience success at publishing, it seems easier to carry on. We would like to offer some suggestions that are helpful for staying motivated. Some of these have been mentioned before, such as dealing with rejection. However, we feel that they bear repeating.

Accept Rejection as Inevitable

There are inevitable blocks and obstacles that will appear on the path. The most inevitable one is rejection. Dealing with rejection is part of being a writer. It seems easiest to expect to be rejected. The theory is that this will help to harden you when rejection does occur. However, Susan once mistakenly sent an article to the wrong journal. She was certain they would reject it but they accepted it! We are not always the best judges of where our work fits best.

Rejection hurts because it's hard not to take personally. One of Susan's colleagues got a rejection letter early in his career that began, "I shriek in horror when I think someone will probably get a doctoral degree with this drivel." He *had* received a doctoral degree with this work and to this day he remembers the exact words and is still wondering who the cruel reviewer was. However, he has long since put the insult behind him. He believed in his own work and sent his "drivel" elsewhere. Six years later, he is well published. One of the secrets to his success was to not get down on himself personally, but to move on.

The best response to rejection is to move on to another journal. This is where the three journal rule fits in well. It starts with the assumption that rejection is a necessary part of the process and allows the writer to continue on. Occasionally however, there is too great a time lag. For this reason, Susan collects any pertinent recent articles that she comes across while an article is out for review; then she can easily update the literature for a quick turnaround.

Stick to a Routine

Robert Boice (1990) offers many excellent suggestions for self motivation in *Professors as Writers*. Boice has done extensive research on why and how people block the writing process. Based on his findings that both successful and non successful writers often find writing unpleasant and tiring, he set up the four step plan to help ease the pain and encourage self motivation. His four steps are as follows:

1. *Automaticity.* Write spontaneously to get started. If you aren't ready take "automatic notes" of the literature, write a generative source or idea quickly on a piece of paper and pretend you are talking aloud to someone.
2. *Externality.* Motivate yourself to continue by using the priority principle. Writing comes first. Boice suggests behavior modification techniques such as not allowing yourself to engage in a valued activity until after you write. No writing, no shower.
3. *Self control.* Identify and write down your self talk. Keep charts of your progress.
4. *Sociality.* Make writing a social activity by sharing your work with others either as a co author or as a constructive reviewer.

Volunteer to Teach a New Course

This may sound like crazy advice for the already overworked professor, but it guarantees that you will have to explore new areas. This way you are forced to view old material through a different lens. Often the best insights come from someone who is not so immersed in a discipline that they cannot see the forest for the trees. In science, many of the most significant discoveries have been made by individuals who were not specialists in the area under question and therefore could see a problem with fresh eyes.

Present a Workshop in Somewhat Unfamiliar Territory

This is another technique where you will really stretch yourself to do something new. One of our more successful colleagues follows this practice of doing workshops in areas slightly outside his expertise. He then "forces" himself to write about the new ideas and the new connections he has made; he then sends out the piece for publication. He has a good success record and suggests to others to never do a presentation without capitalizing on the experience by writing something after.

Send in Proposals for Conferences

Conference presentations will provide you with a forum for trying out new ideas, obtaining feedback, and building contacts with others who share similar interests. Many conference organizers also use a peer review process for selecting proposals and this can provide you with additional feedback on your ideas. Glen uses conferences as a motivating tool. He knows that he will work towards completing a paper in order to meet the conference deadlines and these papers are usually solid drafts that, with a little additional revising, are soon ready for submission. The fact that he likes to travel means that conferences also act as a reward for finishing the paper.

Identify and Prioritize

One good strategy is to often review possible ideas for articles or books and write these down in a list. You may be surprised how many ideas you actually have–and good ideas can be repackaged in many different forms. This is a kind of brainstorming activity that can best be accomplished during a boring but compulsory meeting. See how many ideas you can come up with. One idea may generate another. Then prioritize the list according to the demands the piece would take and your actual interest in writing it. Doing this on a regular basis keeps lots of ideas floating in and seems to help the goal setting process.

Goal Setting

Probably one of the most serious and motivating activities is to set goals. How many articles or books could you realistically expect to get published in the next five years? Add another one, or two, to that total. (Remember you are always capable of much more than you think.) Find a way to remind yourself of your target. Write the number in big letters and post it in a place where you will be forced to encounter it often. Somehow regularly confronting a sign that says "10+ articles" helps to keep motivated to move toward that goal. The mind is an extremely powerful tool. We can make it work in incredible ways for us. We have seen when this strategy somehow helped motivate people to produce beyond their own imaginations. A bit of magic involved, no doubt, but in the world of academic publishing we need all the magic we can get!

Life After Publication

SEEING YOUR NAME IN PRINT for the first time as the author of a scholarly article is a moment that should be celebrated. Find a way to reward yourself for this accomplishment and continue to reward yourself with every paper that is published. At the same time, remember that writing is a process, not an event. Publishing your first paper should be viewed as an important step in an ongoing cycle of scholarly activity. If you have found your own voice once, you can certainly do it again and it is never too early to begin on the next project, perhaps the day after you submit your first paper to a journal.

There are also a number of things that you should consider doing after each paper is published. First, consider a little self promotion. Many universities and colleges have newspapers that list recent faculty publications. Find out how to list your new article in this column so that others in your institution will know that you have published successfully. It might also be a good idea to give a copy of your new article to your department head or dean. Second, thank those who provided you with assistance. Send a copy of the article and a short note of thanks to individuals who may have helped you by commenting on an earlier draft or copy editing the manuscript. Third, consider sending off prints of the article to individuals that you think may be interested in your ideas. If you used Smith's work as a foundation for your paper, perhaps Smith would enjoy reading your article. Since few academics can afford to subscribe to all of the journals that may be relevant to their work and many libraries are reducing the number of subscriptions, do not assume that Smith, or others important in your field, will have already read or seen your paper. Finally, do not forget to update your curriculum vitae and to place a copy of your published paper in your files. This may seem like such an obvious suggestion, but you would be surprised at the number of academics who lose track of their publications and are forced to go digging in the library just to revise their vitae. Tenure and promotion procedures usually mean that you will have to submit copies of your published work, and it is never too early to begin organizing your papers in a binder. Creating a "Published Papers" binder will also mean that you have at least one copy of each article in a safe place just in case you run out of off prints.

Conclusion

OUR OBJECTIVE IN WRITING this manuscript has been to offer a number of suggestions and approaches that we have found useful in our work. We wanted to share our experience with others, in part because we are in the early stages of our careers and we wanted to reassure relatively new scholars that the challenge of academic writing is just that–a challenge that you can meet with a combination of reflection, a personal strategy, and hard work. We remain convinced that anyone who has established the credentials to obtain an academic position also has the skills and abilities to enter the world of scholarly journals.

We have tried to offer a number of strategies or tricks that we have found successful in our own writing, but as you will have noticed, we do not work the same way and we have quite distinct approaches to the writing process. Our common premise is that writers have to find their own voice. The fact that each of us has found our voice in different ways and that we employ somewhat different strategies suggests that there is no one way to succeed in academic writing. You must find the way that is right for you. Consider each of the strategies we have described above, but as you reread the monograph, pick and choose the notions that seem to represent the closest fit to your personal philosophy and approach.

Finally, try not to forget what it was like to be a novice in academic writing. Keep this in mind when you are asked to review manuscripts for scholarly journals or when you become an editor of a journal. More importantly, think about how you can help the newest generation of academic scholars. If you become a successful published author in your field, how can you share what you have learned with those who are just starting? If academic writing, like almost everything else we do, is a learned process, perhaps each of us has a responsibility to share what we have gained from our experience.

References

American Psychological Association. (1994). *Publication Manual of the American Psychological Association* (4th ed.). Washington, DC: APA.

Belenky, M., Clinchy, B., Goldberger, N., & Tarule, J. (1986) *Women's ways of knowing.* New York: Basic Books.

Boice, R. (1990) *Professors as writers: A self help guide to productive writing.* Stillwater, OK: New Forums Press.

Cabell, D.W.E. (1992). *Cabell's directory of publishing opportunities in education* (3rd ed.) (Vols. 1 2). Beaumont, TX: Cabell Publishing.

Chicago Manual of Style (1982) (13th ed.). Chicago: University of Chicago Press.

Davis, B. (1994). Mathematics Teaching: Moving from telling to listening. *Journal of Curriculum and Supervision 9*, 3, 267 283.

Drake, S.M. & Boak, T. (1992). Toward a model for teaching and learning educational research. Paper presented at Canadian Society for Studies in Education, Charl Hetowa, P.E.I.

Goldberg, N. (1986). *Writing down the bones: The writer within.* London: Shambhala.

Goldberg, N. (1993). *Long quiet highway: Waking up in America.* New York: Bantam.

Hollingsworth, S. (1992). Learning to teach through collaborative conversation. *American Educational Research Journal, 29*, 2, 373 404.

Hunsaker, L. & Johnson, M. (1992). Collaborative case study of teacher change. *American Educational Research Journal, 29*, 2, 350 372.

Luey, B. (1990). *Handbook for academic authors.* Cambridge: Cambridge University Press.

Moxley, J. (1992) *Writing and publishing for academic authors.* Lanham, MD: University Press of America.

Simon, R. (1994). *Editors as gatekeepers: Who, what, why and how gets published in the social sciences.* Lanham, MD: Ronman & Littlefield.

Strunk, W. Jr., & White, E.B. (1979). *The elements of style* (3rd ed.) New York: Macmillan.

www.ingramcontent.com/pod-product-compliance
Lightning Source LLC
Chambersburg PA
CBHW061512040426
42450CB00008B/1577